Gabby Duran is autistic. This is a true story about her sometimes painful childhood. Gabby's journey led to fun and success when she discovered Special Olympics. Gabby lives in Austin, Texas. She is now 26 years old. Gabby enjoys sports and Disney movies, which she loves to discuss. She is active in her community, working part-time at a school kitchen. She also attends choir and art classes and still participates in Special Olympics. Gabby began running for exercise two years ago and participated in her first half-marathon in 2019.

AUSTIN MACAULEY PUBLISHERS™
LONDON • CAMBRIDGE • NEW YORK • SHARJAH

Autism Doesn't Stop Me

Gabby Duran

Illustrated by Amanda Zappler

Copyright © Gabby Duran (2020)
Illustrated by Amanda Zappler

All rights reserved. No part of this publication may be reproduced, distributed, or transmitted in any form or by any means, including photocopying, recording, or other electronic or mechanical methods, without the prior written permission of the publisher, except in the case of brief quotations embodied in critical reviews and certain other non-commercial uses permitted by copyright law. For permission requests, write to the publisher.

Any person who commits any unauthorized act in relation to this publication may be liable to criminal prosecution and civil claims for damages.

Ordering Information:
Quantity sales: special discounts are available on quantity purchases by corporations, associations, and others. For details, contact the publisher at the address below.

Publisher's Cataloging-in-Publication data
Duran, Gabby and Zappler, Amanda
Autism Doesn't Stop Me

ISBN 9781647502362 (Paperback)
ISBN 9781647502379 (Hardback)
ISBN 9781647502386 (ePub e-book)

Library of Congress Control Number: 2020903263

www.austinmacauley.com/us

First Published (2020)
Austin Macauley Publishers LLC
40 Wall Street, 28th Floor
New York, NY 10005
USA
mail-usa@austinmacauley.com
+1 (646) 5125767

Dedicated to my friends and family. Some of them understood me before and some, I hope, will understand me now.

This book is a true story written by Gabby Duran, who grew up in Texas with autism spectrum disorder and what that was like.

I grew up in Austin, Texas. My favorite animals were jaguars and hedgehogs.

When I was a little girl, I loved playing with my best friend, Gray, who was quiet like me.

Even before I went to school, I wanted to play with other kids, but I only talked a little and most kids spoke too fast for me.

Autism made it really hard to talk and make friends. Sometimes I watched the other kids having fun on the playground and playing kickball. I wanted to join them so badly.

I made only a few friends in school and it hurt my feelings when kids left me out.

Sometimes teachers talked too much and too fast and I couldn't understand them. In middle school, the resource room geography teacher sent me to a Life Skills Special Ed classroom even though it was too easy for me. My teachers did not always understand me.

My choir teacher encouraged me though and I cut up a little bit with friends I made in my Life Skills classroom. I enjoyed school in the Life Skills and Resource rooms where I felt good about myself.

I loved the cartoon Sponge Bob, and I wanted to catch jelly fish!

I loved birthday parties and getting together with friends and family.

I lived at home with my mom, dad, and my little sister (who was my best friend). I had a dog named Murphy; my dad's dog, Kolben; and our cat, Cupcake. I always loved animals.

My family went to the beach every summer and we even took a trip to Walt Disney World one time.

I had dreams of going to more places, and traveling far away, but I didn't like flying that much.

My favorite holiday was Thanksgiving but I loved Christmas too!

I watched the Disney movies so many times that I memorized them! I enjoyed drawing Dalmatians.

I loved my art classes and I drew a snowman after going to Philadelphia for Christmas one year.

I rode a special ed. bus to school, which was smaller than the other buses.

I got enrolled in Special Olympics and collected lots of medals.

I started participating in all kinds of sports through Special Olympics and other inclusive programs. I finally got to play Kickball!

No one wants to be left out and Special Olympics helped me to belong.

I loved my friends and always included them.

I loved my teachers and my school.

CPSIA information can be obtained
at www.ICGtesting.com
Printed in the USA
LVHW011055291020
670026LV00006B/159